P9-BYL-009

GLORIA

Children's Books

Nihil Obstat, Arthur J. Scanlan, S.T.D., Censor Liborum
Imprimatur ✠ Francis Cardinal Spellman,
Archbishop of New York
Cum Permissu Superiorum

William J. Hirten Co., Cumberland, RI

GLORIA
Children's Books

The Story of Mary

Our Mother

by Daniel A. Lord, S.J.

This is the story of the sweetest
woman that ever lived.
She is called the Blessed Mother.
Her name is Mary,
but we all know her because
she is our dear Mother in Heaven.
The first woman's name was Eve.
She too was beautiful and good.
But many long years after,
a little girl was born.
She was sweet and pure.
She loved God very much.
She disliked sin and would have nothing
to do with God's enemy.

From the very beginning, her soul was
more beautiful than the
loveliest angel's.
God the Father looked at her and said,
"This is my sweet daughter."
God the Holy Spirit looked at her and said,
"This is my pure little bride."
God the Son looked at her and said,
"I want her to be my Mother."
So Mary became the purest woman
that ever lived.
Later on she said of herself,
"I am the Immaculate Conception."

Mary lived in a little house with
Ann her mother,
and Joachim, her Father.
She was a good obedient little girl.
She went to church on the Sabbath.
She helped her mother
around the house.
She was gentle and good to
all her friends.
God loved her very much
because she loved God very much.
She had a very nice childhood and
grew up to be a fine young woman.

So one day God sent
His Angel Gabriel to visit her.
The Angel knelt before her.
He saw how beautiful she was,
and how full of love and faith
and virtue her soul was.
He said, "Hail, full of grace."
Then he told her that she was going
to be God's Mother.
So Mary answered,
"Behold the handmaid of the Lord.
Be it done unto me according to your word."
That meant: "I would like to be God's
little servant and take care of Him.
Whatever God wants, I want."
Mary became the Mother of God.

Mary was married to a very good man
named Joseph. An angel told him that his wife was
going to be the Mother of God.
He was very glad and promised to take
care of her and her dear little Son.
One cold night, Mary was taken
by Joseph to Bethlehem.
Mary and Joseph were very poor.
They had no money to pay for
a decent hotel room.
The inns were crowded and the innkeepers
said rudely, "No room! No room!"
So Mary was taken to a stable
in the side of the hill.
It was cold and barren.
Only animals lived there.
But Mary made it beautiful with
her love and her work.

And there she was given her
precious little Son, Jesus.
The Angels came from heaven to sing in joy.
They knew that the little Baby in Mary's
arms was the Son of God.
The Shepherds ran to see the Baby,
and Mary showed Him to them.
They cried aloud in happiness.
Three Wise Men saw a new Star in the East,
and came to kneel before
the little Son of Mary.
They called Him the King of Kings.
Mary loved her little Baby and
held Him close to her heart.
She was very, very happy.
For this was the first Christmas.

Mary took care of the house for Joseph
and her little Son.
She cooked the meals and did the wash.
She taught Jesus His lessons.
And even though He was God,
He did just what His mother wanted.
Mary took her Son with her to the bazaars.
She often looked out the window and
watched Him play.
She rocked Him to sleep when He was little.
Then when He was a grown man,
she kissed Him goodbye.
She saw Him leave her little house to go out
and take care of His Father's business.
Mary was very lonely, but she was so
glad that Jesus was her strong, fine Son.

She listened when He told
the people about Heaven.
She was delighted when He raised
the dead to life and healed the sick.
She heard of the wonderful things He did,
and knew this was her wonderful Son.
Mary was the first one to believe in Jesus.
Mary served Him with all her strength.
She knew He was the Son of God
She was happy because He
was always her beloved Son.

Then Mary heard things that
made her sad and afraid.
She heard that bad men did not love her Son.
They hated Him because
He was good to the people.
They came up with a plan to kill Him.
Mary wished she could help her Son.
She would gladly have given
her life to save Him.
But she knew He had to die for sinners.
One night Mary heard terrible news.
The soldiers had come and arrested Him.
They had dragged Him away to prison.
They had brought Him to Pontius
Pilate who ordered Him to die.

Poor Mary! She saw her dear Son
carrying His Cross up the road of Calvary.
She could not help Him.
She could only suffer with Him.
When they nailed her dear Son to the Cross
and lifted the Cross up high,
she took her place beneath it.
She could not wipe His forehead;
because He was raised too high.
When He was dead, she held out her
arms to receive Him.
She took Him to her heart.
She washed His poor, beaten body.
She dressed Him for the grave.
She loved Him until death.
That is why we call
Mary the Mother of Sorrows.

23

Mary knew that her Son was God.
She knew He would rise from the grave.
So she waited for the First Easter.
And when the sun rose,
He rose strong and immortal.
He came to His Mother and
took her in His grateful arms.
Mary was very happy.
Her Son lived once more.
He would never die again.
She knew that He was King of all the world.
Then her Son went up to Heaven.
She saw Him rise from the mount.

But, even though she was
lonesome without Him,
she stayed to help His friends, the Apostles.
She was the Mother of the Church and
the Queen of the Apostles.
When Mary was a dear old lady, she died.
The Apostles buried her.
The next day they visited her grave.
It was open.
Where the body of Mary had rested,
beautiful lilies and roses bloomed.
Jesus had taken the body of
His Mother to Heaven.
We must never forget that even though
she is the Mother of God,
She is our dear Mother too.